Trancelumination

Trancelumination

John Bradley

Lowbrow
Press

Einleitung

TRANCELUMINATION
Copyright 2011 John Bradley

All rights reserved. Published in the United States of America.

No part of this book may be reproduced or transmitted in any form, or by any means, electronic or mechanical, including but not limited to photocopying, recording or by any information storage or retrieval system without written permission from the publisher.

Cover design: Jeff Peterson

Published by Lowbrow Press
www.lowbrowpress.com

ISBN 978-0-9829553-7-6

In the beginning
was the Word
and the Word
was "Um."

– Anonymous

For Jana

*she who needs
no aphorism*

CONTENTS

On The Need for Something
Like an Aphorism   **21**

I	**23**
II	**35**
III	**41**
IV	**53**
V	**65**
VI	**77**
VII	**89**
VII	**97**

On the Need for Something Like an Aphorism

I make friends with my shirt, taking it out to lunch and then a stroll, as I was taught to do in Social Studies, though I still don't know whether to address my companion with "Your Excellency" or "Hey, Dude." Because my father told me as I came into this world to be sure to get a haircut regularly and I'd be able to sell the dirt behind my ears. She made a book out of slices of Wonder Bread, with watermelon seeds for words and punctuation. When I invented the runcible shovel, I had no idea so much of the world consists of liquid. As a weathered garage imbibes a paint called portal blue, I can only utter: "Levitate, ye latex leviathan." One of my nipples, the worldly one I've been told, is famous, though I admit it bothers me to no end that I can't say which is which. He tossed into the lake the bicycle she had ridden to and from on, with an egg on her head, because, he explained, he couldn't bear to see the world balanced so precariously. Rhubarb demands I get down on my knees, place an ear to one of its shaggy leaves, and listen. She kissed me, in front of the herd of flamingos, thus causing me to feel to this day an erotic attraction to cinema. I nibble on my fingernails; how can I condemn the miserable rats; the edge of the world frays.

I

trancelumination:

to glow unawares,
to cast light across a surly distance.

I wake to blue jay squawk, and think: "I-blue-to-wake-think-squawk."

❧

Each voiceprint bears a trace of the Big Bang.

❧

Smoke needs no passport.

❧

Oh, to live in a nation where the currency says, plain and naked, "In Grub, We Trust."

❧

Warning: I sleep in boiled roots.

❦

NO MOTORIZED
UTTERANCES
BEYOND
THIS POINT

❦

Here's everything I know about love: Eros prefers a fork, and I a spoon or spork.

❦

Lecturing a class of adults at Prairieview Community College on Ezra Pound, I realize I haven't had a chance to prepare the lecture, but I do recall the central events of Pound's life—his years riding with General George Armstrong Custer. How Pound was really a spy for Crazy Horse all along, hence Custer's humiliating defeat at Little Big Horn. How late in Pound's life he disclosed that all of his poems were part of a single work entitled: *White Buffalo Calf Woman Cantos*. That was why he was able to tolerate Custer's infantile practical jokes and addiction to Cheetos, which were sent daily from the East by carrier pigeon. Pound secretly recorded it all, every wind-tossed bag of Cheetos, every slain buffalo grandmother or grandfather. "If poetry can't bring about the coming of the white buffalo, then why bother?" Pound told Crazy Horse one night beneath an I-80 overpass. It is not known whether Crazy Horse accepted

Pound's gift of a bag of Cheetos. I close the lecture with Pound's most famous poem, written in Dodge City's infamous Metro Hotel, in the underground opium den:
> The apparition of white buffalo on the plains;
> Petals on a wet, black plow.

◉

Picture a bird's wing on the side of a cat and you're close.

◉

Without love or malice, kiss your collarbone at least once a day.

◉

The vowel in a turbulent car flooded with rutting microbes is still a vowel.

❧

If you condone the curvaceousness of spaghetti, how can you bark at NO PARKING signs?

❧

Just because you were born in Brooklyn doesn't mean your nipples were too.

❧

Warning: Reading *Dr. Zhivago* while traveling may induce the desire to place high in a large, leafy tree a large round glass ball.

❧

Ask a penis anything and it will answer with a sigh.

Listening to a white German shepherd muzzy with motor oil barking in the moonlit garage: noise is all we have left of God.

If you ignore the smell of my poetics, I'll ignore the smell of your politics.

Photo by John Cohen, New York City, 1962: a baby-faced kid in newsboy cap, tousled work shirt, baggy dark pants sagging over his scuffed black work boots. Impish schoolboy look on his face, as if we caught him just after he took a whiz in the alley. Question: How did this scruffy kid ever become Bob Dylan?

Carry the fruit or the worm, your choice, but carry something.

In Paris, I was once served an aphorism covered with fresh raspberries and drizzled with dark chocolate.

Flatter the bullet but praise the potato.

When warts invaded the back of my hand, I let the generals use the tactic that defeated Napoleon: scorched earth. But a wart, I discovered, is far smarter than Napoleon.

In the event of erratum, violate the social norm of your choice.

❧

I once met Bettie Page on a rainy Thursday in downtown Tuscaloosa. She was wearing a black raincoat, sunglasses, and hid her hair in a black kerchief. "Did you see that cockroach climbing up the leg of the store mannequin?" I asked. "I've always wanted to hear someone say that," she replied.

❧

Miss a messenger and the gears, the gears keep grinding the clouds into flour.

❧

Beware the Six and a Half Laws of Aphorisms: 1. You'll never learn what time it is from an aphorism, but you can see the moon through the "o." 2. An aphorism may give you a splinter though you never touch it. 3. The aphorist must always sound like he or she is fully clothed. 4. Never perform brain surgery while under the influence of an aphorism. 5. An aphorism may be made of rags and sawdust, yet it promises stardust. 6. If you think you're still the same after partaking of an aphorism, it somehow succeeded. 6a. If it succeeds, then it cannot be a true aphorism.

👁

Tilt my head back until I can see that hole in the sky where your eye watches me watch you tilting my head back.

👁

Rain speaks many dialects, yet no one ever requires a translator.

👁

I can smell the truth on your fingers. But not my own.

👁

Warning: This ladder won't reach the top, or the lowest root, of the mulberry tree.

❧

Water forgives anything, even those who slurp it.

❧

You thought you said, "Tiny burdens of salt." I thought I heard "The tide buries us all."

❧

And to think it all began with a cloud shaped like a ball-peen hammer.

II

trancelumination:

that moment when you notice your father lurking in the back of the room wearing the brown sweater with an argyle stripe running up each sleeve. He looks disturbed. You pull him aside and ask what's troubling him. "Someone has stored tires in my bed," he says.

Lines for the fortune cookies:

Look, I've got other things to do besides peer into your cavernous future.

Your lunch break is almost over and I still don't know how to tell you this.

You will read this and still leave your hat behind.

Did you try the duck? In orange glaze? You would have liked it.

I'm supposed to say something bluntly elliptical and you're supposed to be mildly intrigued.

You should be reading Apollinaire.

Why deny it? You've loved more than anyone you have ever known.

Imagine a world with no cars or trusses.

No one wants to hear bad news, so let's just say you won't be going this year to Tangier.

Ok, it's been fun, but now back to wordlessness.

You will write a book with a Q-tip and Vaseline and then paint a painting with a q-tip and Vaseline and then be endowed by the q-tip and Vaseline syndicate.

I've wasted another perfectly good Tuesday on you.

All right, all right—your rich aunt will choke on a cherry stone and leave her millions to you and her stuffed cat.

If you see Kenneth, tell him poets don't throw the best parties. Bees do.

You will write "altar" when you mean to write "alter" and no one will notice.

Somebody peed on the front steps. You will find a job.

Please don't toss me into the sweet and sour sauce.

You could be watching *Mothra vs. The Little Tramp*.

Don't believe your lover—Oprah *did* read every one of those Oprah book picks.

You will light a candle made of beef and smell lilac and Rolaids.

Sipping a sazerac in the bathtub cannot be unhealthy.

Sappho of Lesbos, your table is ready.

Aren't you supposed to be eating your fortune cookie right about now?

One day someone will ask you for your autograph and you will write

"The night has no street address and yet I always seem to find it."

Well, Kent Johnson, who the hell do you think wrote this?

The sun sees only what the dust of the moon allows it to see.

You try writing fortunes a penny each and see what *you* come up with.

How soon you will forget this in the great circumpolar darkness.

Even if you read this in bed, it won't make you any wiser.

Sure you will fall into an Irish bog, but you'll meet your beloved in the intensive care unit.

One day you will be a statue and strangers will rub your ass for good luck.

You should be reading Frank O'Hara.

III

trancelumination:

*to wear red socks and white shoes;
to speak ill of another's footwear.*

"After you," says the Possible to the Impossible. "No, after you," says the Impossible to the Possible. "I hate the impossibly polite," says the Possible to the Impossible. "I despise the possibly urbane," says the Impossible to the Possible. "That's quite impossible," says the Possible to the Impossible. "Sounds rather probable," says the Impossible to the Possible. "Unbelievable," says the Possible to the Impossible. "All too likely," says the Impossible to the Possible. Downstairs someone breaks a femur.

👁

Warning: I sleep on moving objects.

👁

A list believes the Buddha resides in everything.

👁

"The only person I trust is my accountant," he told me. "And I don't even trust her."

◉

I pet the cat, and her fur glows blue. Was it something in my hand, some chemical reaction? Or had her fur been blue before I ever pet her? I follow her movements, watching for some small gesture to let me know she's slipping into raccoon, snail, broom. She knows I'm watching, so she flops down on the newspaper and purrs gray.

◉

Tuning fork or song fish? Choose your weapon carefully.

◉

"Politics don't appeal to me. I don't like people who don't care about the truth," he tells me. I nod. How do I tell him his statement leads directly to the door with the sign that reads: "Quiet. Interrogation in Progress."

◉

To translate dirt, you need a spoon, a length of rubber hose, and a taste for the mundane.

◉

Motion makes its own music.

◉

Speak only bent vowels to an unguent.

◉

Warning: These words may fluoresce if read on the Sea of Tranquility.

❂

Says a resident of Arles recalling the canvases of Vincent Van Gogh: "They all stunk of sweat and onions."

❂

The sparrow that built its nest inside the fire alarm has no need of a fire extinguisher.

❂

Why aphorisms should never be allowed to congregate in groups larger than one: My father's expensive-but-on-sale shoe, the one with the razor-slit he made for his little toe to peek out. The charge receipt (for a plate of waffles with strawberries) signed by Jason Robards she keeps at all times on her person. That scene in *Yesterday, Today, and Tomorrow* where Sophia Loren does her infamous striptease ("Only a Catholic could strip like that," noted her husband). The white towel stuffed inside my chest, to fill the cantaloupe-size hole there beneath my shirt. My brother calling to ask whether he should bet on the Chicago Bears the money hid in his freezer. She, on the ladder, painting goldfish on the ceiling; me, just below, hand heating the rung, daring her ankle to brush my ear. What I found in my pocket for the homeless man blocking the door to the train station: a cowboy hat that fits snug on a thumb. The letter my mother writes to Sister Clara explaining why I failed to write the required twenty vocabulary words twenty thousand times each. The tact squad practicing their Harmon Killibrew swings, their hardwood clubs smacking the telephone pole on Cedar Avenue. My brother calling to ask if I was sure the Bears would lose, and by twenty-three points. That black olive I tugged from the branch, in Mijas, to learn something about the mortality of angels. The scent of Frida's tortilla painting—of her monkey painting a portrait of Frida on a tortilla—a hint of lime, groin, geranium.

👁

He smoked five packs of Marlboros a day, and he jogged five miles a day, each proving the possibility of the other.

👁

The heron violates only the laws not made by the heron.

👁

Electricity has no kin.

❦

It's not that difficult to levitate a potato, but would you really want to eat a spud that's once been severed from gravity?

❦

Drawing a watch and band on his wrist, he suffused the room with time.

❦

The source of the Nile was located today in a toilet at Grand Central.

❦

Don't perch on the back porch reading Antonio Porchia, unless you don't mind purchasing a pomegranate with your corpse.

◉

No good storyteller was ever born with only ten toes.

◉

On the flight to Baghdad, a woman with a box of animal crackers sits next to me. Curious, I ask if they are a gift for a child in Iraq. "Oh, no! They're poisoned," she confesses. A kindly gentleman had asked her to transport the crackers, but told her not to eat them or she would suffer greatly. "But why not let him carry his own poison crackers?" I ask. "Oh, poor man," she replies. He's allergic to the them."

◉

To translate a spoonful of silence, forceps and a cloth damp with starlight is required.

◉

He could read the broken shell but not the unbroken egg.

❂

She asked if she could borrow my tiny burden of salt, as hers were becoming much too easy to bear.

❂

I'd prefer you didn't open your rib cage in front of strangers.

❂

A shirt of woven wind should never be worn with lead pants laced with fire.

❂

Lying underneath the dining room table, I understood for the first time why I must write *An Encyclopedia of Clouds*.

👁

Warning: On casual Friday, don't wear socks spun from human flesh.

👁

"You could beat me with a cloud," he said, so that's exactly what we did.

👁

The fire left little purple stars all over her body, which made us love her even more, which made her love us even less.

IV

trancelumination:

*to compulsively draw eyes on the back
of someone's shaved head.*

Sign on the front desk at the library: "Silence spoken here."

◉

When you bring the linen napkin to your lips in the dining car of a west bound train, salt no longer clots in the salt shaker.

◉

The photograph of someone in Duluth older than an elm should not be left in a room with a figurine from Prague.

◉

Gunpowder and black pepper and saliva and a bolt of black silk: They cannot constitute a crow. Though it is difficult, on a gray day, to discern the difference.

◉

Each time a hair is cut, a wooden bird takes flight. But if you must shave your head, rinse your scalp with a warm pitcher of cold milk.

◉

Drop a burning book from a stone bridge, if you wish to find the hole in the sock of your beloved.

◉

Never use a semicolon, she told me, where a ballet slipper will do.

◉

Perhaps the semicolon should be named, more appropriately, the semicomma. It doesn't quite signal the end of anything, nor is it absolutely certain something new is about to begin. Rather, like its cousin the comma, it seems to rest in a constant state of uncertainty. The lower half of the semicolon, that is the comma, swings loosely, like a lantern, casting its frail light out over the night grass. The light claims dominion over the night, but when the lantern swings back, the dark rushes in. The upper half, the period floating over the comma, can be said to resemble a telescope. If you peer through it long enough, you can see a fire far off. Some unknown intruder inadvertently set fire to some dry grass, and it quickly spread to the surrounding forest, now burning out of control. Some say the fire is spreading in this direction. But that's all very far away and of no concern to the semicolon.

◉

As I entered her tent, she was playing a recently discovered piece by Vivaldi on an oboe made with grasshopper wings and crickets.

◉

When sounds of gunfire are heard after making love, write a letter beginning: "Everything tends toward passion."

◉

If I say, "This is George weather," you'll assume there must be a George. I'm a George, or you're a George. Or George is a George.

❖

A photograph of an open mouth reminds me of the space between the rungs of a ladder.

❖

The novel of a friend is always much better or much worse than expected.

❖

The poet says, "The best poem has no need of words." The lexicographer says, "No poem deserves its words." The cartographer says, "Every poem is an attempt to speak the unknown."

❖

Whoever invented the pocket attempted to make up for the body's deficiency.

The driver in the car with a canoe on the roof needs no hat.

In my high-backed office chair my father still pilots his white Chrysler New Yorker with the hailstone dings.

Everything I know about the architecture of the sentence, I learned at the lecture on the uses of petroleum jelly.

In the People's Court of Reversed Justice, the custodian sits in the robe of the judge, and the lawyer sweeps up.

❂

I saw Ratko Mladic at a poetry reading. He sat in the back row, arms crossed, with a baseball cap pulled low over his eyes. He applauded loudly at inappropriate times. I wonder. Did his parents, when he was an infant, call him Baby Rat?

❂

After I stole Lady Gaga's toothbrush, she told me, "Nothing complements you like your own grave."

❂

One of those Tuesdays that arrives out of an oboe on Wednesday.

❂

Ask a bullet what it thinks of lettuce, and you'll never eat a salad again.

"I don't believe in the color purple," said the man with black fingernails. "I only believe in the bruised who dance."

Warning: I may at unannounced moments sit in a clump of chicory and declare: "This is my throne."

The square was invented by the military, the circle by a poet, the eraser by an anarchist.

I'm a step on a three-step ladder. I'm just not sure which one.

◉

No matter how dire, how horrid the news, the BBC newscasters stay unruffled, their voices a cool music. "Tell me more," they make me plead.

◉

I had to scrape snow and ice off the push buttons before I could dial. Then the operator said, "Are you sure you meant to call London?" "I'd like to speak to Don Paterson, the aphorist," I explained. "Oh, that Scottish bloke. He has us route all his calls to a plumber who goes by the name Don Paterson. So why bother? Cheers." Then the sweet sound of dial tone.

◉

After laughter or sex, the muscles in the face relax.

◉

The ant in the frying pan can no longer recall the taste of the desert.
◉

The doctor dried her hands in the etherized patient's hair.

◉

I placed my ear over the speck of blood on my pillow only to hear its alibi.

V

trancelumination:

*to marry a loaf of braided bread
as it reminds you of your beloved.*

I made a list of everything I love. Then a list of everything I find annoying. They were exactly the same.

◉

Julie Christie inquired through her lawyer why I had her name tattooed on my ankle. "Why wasn't my name tattooed on hers?" I replied.

◉

At the Institute of Erotic Studies, my mother is the one who asks, "Now what is it exactly you do here?"

◉

Without the constant wheeling of blood, these words flicker and ash.

❂

The children of Caliban have never heard of Caliban.

❂

Poetic justice: The man who designed the AK-47 died from acid reflux.

❂

Only rain believes every word of *The Book of Fire*.

❂

From *The Book of Arson*: I never set a book of Chinese poetry translated into French on fire. I never knowingly set my serge trousers, or anyone else's, on fire. I never set fire to a mannequin that had a cockroach crawling up her left leg. I never carved the word FIRE into the flesh of a watermelon. I never spelled the word FIRE using matchsticks or French fries. I never found a pair of dusty serge trousers by the railroad tracks and then set them on fire. I never set a long-haired dog or long-haired cat on fire. I never set a ladybug or a long ladder on fire. I never set a can of soup on fire with lighter fluid. I never set a plate of freshly boiled angel hair pasta on fire. I never set an exhausted carpet in a movie theater balcony on fire, ever. I never wrote the word "FIRE" on a mirror with a bar of soap in the men's or women's room. I never set a book of Cuban poetry that was translated into English on fire, though the pages appeared singed by intense heat. I never set a Bible on fire, though I have seen one burning near a levee and watched two men put the fire out by urinating on it. I never knowingly transported fire across a finish line, though I did haul a sofa that had once been in a fire across a state line for a friend. I never set a spider on fire, even one with a nest behind the toilet, though I was asked to once by a person whose name I will not mention as she died recently in a most unfortunate fire. I never visited the woman and poured a jar of fire ants on her grave. I never intentionally set fire to my own bed, though I do recall sitting on a Greyhound bus, watching a crow pick up a burning cigarette from the sidewalk, the same cigarette that had been in my mouth just seconds before now clenched in its smoking black beak. I never intended to be a volunteer fireman. I just know where the fire is going to be before the fire does, that's all.

◉

"Torpor" can also mean "to be aware your veins and arteries can clearly be seen by anyone who cares to notice."

◉

"Someday I'm going to plant a match and watch fire blossom," said a farmer to his wife. Said the farmer's wife, "In the rocky field of grammar."

❧

As if mouth music could still the grass thrashing about in the throbbing wind.

❧

Fallen off the Georgia map: Po Biddy Crossroads, Dewy Rose, Cloudland, Hemp, Experiment, Sharp Top, Roosterville, Retreat, Chatoogaville, Hickory Level, Due West, Poetry Tulip, Hope You Like It.

❧

Every seventh year, place all your literal aphorisms into a mortar, and grind them gently with your figurative pestle.

❧

Yet to be digested into aphorism: "Civilians have borne the brunt of modern war with ten civilians dying for every soldier in wars since the mid-twentieth century compared with nine soldiers killed for every civilian in WWI" (*New York Times*, 10/23/10).

◉

The voice emerging from your elbow is not necessarily your elbow's voice.

◉

But I prefer to brush my teeth with an older Frenchman.

◉

Never floss the teeth of a visiting relative.

❧

Sign your name with carrot, turnip, cucumber, zucchini, but never crucifix.

❧

From *Soap: A Brief History*: She opened her suitcase in Dublin to find she had packed a bar of Irish Spring.

❧

On our very first date, Laura Nyro let me place a black rose on her damp crucifix.

❧

The guy with the 12-pack of Miller Lite hears the Polish accent of the clerk and says to her, "Are you Polish?" "That's an invasion of my privacy," the clerk responds. "I was just curious," he says. And she gives him a litany of things he could be curious about: the weather, the Cubs, the cost of stupidity. "My parents, they're Polish . . ," he offers in defense. The clerk continues to scold him. After he leaves, she tells me, "I didn't mean to remove his kidney," wiping her bloody hand on her shirt.

❖

Only someone who never swallowed a bird's nest could say that.

❖

Overheard in Fort Collins, Colorado: "But the rose is thicker than the thorn."

❖

Matter is larger than nothing but always smaller than something.

❦

You: Rub your face where a bit of my spit throbs. I: Touch my face where your face burns. You: Point a finger at my saliva center. I: Close my mouth and close it again. My: Heart pounds at the bottom of my feet. You tell me: "The world began in spittle and in spittle it will end."

❦

She took me through a humid laundromat where washed and unwashed clothes looked all the same. We emerged in a field where Emily Dickinson was buried. I wonder how they carried her body through the laundromat.

❦

He went on and on about Zen. I stared at the tiny wet spot below his fly.

❦

On that bathroom sink beached in the back of the garage, someone painted, using only tinctures of oyster blue, a small island. In the center of the island, on a slight rise, two figures, one white, smudged with blue, the other blue, smudged with white, commingle at the core, while behind them, just below the three drainage holes in the back of the sink, two birds, one blue, smudged with white, the other white, smudged with blue, burst from the island in a flurry of panic closely related to states of common rapture.

◉

Lot 364: Gandhi Items: glasses, leather sandals, philtrum, brass bowl, pocket watch, and silver slingshot.

◉

If only I could read the words rising and falling beneath these words.

VI

trancelumination:

*to harness the energy in a moving tongue,
preferably someone else's.*

At the party, the Rabbits were caught nibbling on Mr. and Mrs. Cabbage's firm green flesh. Mr. and Mrs. Cabbage pretended nothing was wrong, while Mr. and Mrs. Rabbit, glassy eyed, apologized. "This will never, ever happen again," said the Rabbits, drooling slightly as they chewed the lush, juicy flesh of the Cabbages.

⬩

Inside the devil's dildo, a termite dreams.

⬩

The signature of the ant and the elephant are often confused.

⬩

If I must fly, then it's in an airplane made of birds.

👁

The atoms in the owl remember the owl in every atom.

👁

Ill-mannered rats make me nervous.

👁

Never dine on someone else's shadow.

👁

Lettuce usually let's us.

◉

"Sprinkle cumin upon your celery," proclaims a noted author, "so you'll never develop a taste for celebrity."

◉

We know so much about tofu, and yet so little about the Infinite Toad.

◉

From *A History of Clouds:* The mold in the kitchen cupboard softly ticking. The three toes at the bottom of the potato sack. The chicken bone on the saucer curling against the empty coffee cup. The sparrow with the small, egg-shaped songs in its chest. The principal who no one will tell has a slice of burnt toast on his right shoulder. The musician on the flight from Phoenix who knows, from the basil scent of the woman's hair in the seat ahead, he must compose a song for four saxophones and a kettle drum. The continents of water on the flat rooftop of the store that sells guns and tapes of the Elvis impersonator born in Iran. The pointed-toed shoe once used to stir a can of silver paint. The boy with a trombone case filled with the feathers he found along the riverbank. The first and the second and the third time the man in the Burger King orders French fries without remembering he just placed an order for French fries. The Greyhound bus traveling across Nebraska, each moment drawing nearer to Minneapolis without ever leaving Nebraska. The heavy luminescence around a missile underneath the prairie where a woman once played her flute for a sick buffalo. The whale who swallowed the hair of a violinist who lives in Tokyo and at that moment chokes on her glass of water. The AIDS patient who sees, each time he falls asleep, a hand wiping numbers off a white sign above the stack of green crates filled with clean glasses. The grinding of a root against a buried gas tank. The pilot who carries at all times a book, translated from the Chinese, entitled *The History Of Clouds*. My mother, in her long, turquoise bathrobe, wandering from room to room, trying to find the basement door.

❂

Flashing across the electronic message board on the vending machine that dispensed novels: "BREAK IN CASE OF NARRATIVE DISRUPTION."

❂

Why Americans can't get Italian art: "Venus was given a new hand and Mars was given a new penis."

❂

"The whole is always more than any part," states the sentence. "The part is always more than the whole," sighs the fragment.

[Leave space here for the passing of oblivion.]

What not to do Saturday morning: Look out the window and see yourself taking out the trash.

I'd rather push a boxcar through a row of poplars than be seen wearing a leather harness.

Whoever points to a sparrow celebrates an implement of husbandry.

❂

The shoebox full of cilantro carried from room to room had only one alibi and it smelled like cilantro.

❂

OK, who stole the battery from the twenty-seventh letter of the alphabet?

❂

In lieu of an aphorism on Jackson Pollock's hairpiece: She said she'd seen my brother's gravestone in the spaghetti aisle, I caught myself sprinkling chili pepper on the cat's food, a tiny hole in my shirt where my left nipple bobs. I will not be surprised when you are poured into my hand, inhaling Coltrane's "Naima" from a brown paper bag, a speck of blood on the side of the toilet paper roll. All my films are handheld clothesline documentaries, sawing the moon into narrow strips, sewing the walls together with arsenic thread. I have a great fear of bathtub anthropologists, gelid green soup in an Omaha Chinese restaurant, the karaoke singer forging a country-western version of "Desolation Row." My father's veins shot every three weeks with impacted ice, we have yet to suck the vowels from my brother's tongue, the vacuum cleaner left running at the car wash. I paint the picket fence with a turkey baster, a skeleton woman gives birth to a skeleton baby, guess the number of doggie biscuits in the glass jar. Comma splices plug the sink and toilet, a pencil cannot support the weight of the Ark, the full moon through the bullet hole in the landing window. Yes, black ants waltz in the harvest wheat field, Paul McCartney snorts Rilke every chance he gets, fingertips read the rash on the back of my mother's hand. Aunt Betty stubs her cigarette out on one of my tomato plants, Dolly Parton pulling FBI documents from my cleavage, a film you can only see when it's projected upon back and thigh. So you went bowling with Jackson Pollock, pollinating with Bowling Jackson, water boarding again and again in Jackson Hole.

◉

Joni Mitchell won't remember this, I'm sure, but absorbed in a conversation with a Russian reporter she took the aphorism off the tip of her tongue and placed it on mine.

◉

How soon I grew dizzy in the Hall of the Immortals, vomiting behind the white marble bust of Catullus.

◉

But that's not a poem," she insisted. "It's lime Jell-O cast in the shape of a skull."

❂

All the way to Japan, he remembered the car in the airport parking lot with the headlights dimming into daylight.

❂

Sighing blue water rising into sighing blue sky. Blue of a Japanese woodblock print. Silent birdhouse balancing on motionless pole. Or is it a pole balancing a prayer to the goddess of falling leaves? Two women, visibly related to the other in their labor, raking, side by side. Backs bent, hands trusting the bamboo of bamboo pole, they disappear into their task. Will there be smoked fish for lunch? Can raking be seen as conducting a concerto underneath the earth only by one who is not raking? Gazing at their bent backs, am I in some way responsible for holding them to their labor? Shadows gather on the narrow branches like black robes found under snow.

❂

No one can explain why, right before the blizzard, my father took Wite-Out to the stripes of the zebra.

"But something's missing," said Something Missing. "Are you something found or something else?" said Something Else. "But something is not everything," said But Everything. "Yet something's still missing," said Something Missing. "That and something else," said Something Else. "But not everything," said But Everything. That's when I noticed the small willow tree growing from my foot.

VII

trancelumination:

*to stare at an object—an eggplant, say—until it glows,
to confuse light with glowing darkness.*

From an unscientific survey in response to the question "What is (if there is) Midwest poetry?"

Carl Sandburg: "I asked the professors who teach the meaning of meaning and they told me about their lawns."

Lorine Niedecker: "I was born where I was born water borne."

Jeff Tweedy: "Who gave you my email address?"

Former Illinois Governor George Ryan: "You won't believe all the poems I've been writing since I got here."

Lisel Mueller: "It must have a belly button and an anus."

Arielle Greenberg: "Did you know that Kafka washed his hands before he went to the bathroom?"

Nin Andrews: "An orgasm knows no east nor west."

Vachel Lindsay: "Boomlay, boomlay, boomlay, Boom."

Edgar Lee Masters: "They still read Spoon River? Really?"

James Tate: "I think it's now made in China."

Lucien Stryk (Or Possibly Shinkichi Takahashi): "Don't wear argyle socks at a convention of arsonists."

Lorine Niedecker: "In a spoon in a church in a janitor's closet in a spool of thread on the edge of a hospital bed on the spine of a book of do-it-yourself plumbing repair."

Robert Bly: "Wasn't that you in the hammock on Duffy's farm?"

Meridel LeSeuer: "Ask the corn. Ask the milkweed. Ask the idiot who keeps asking the same thing over and over."

Bob Dylan: "A democracy of the tired and weary."

Jim Harrison: "I dreamed that I dreamed I was giving birth to a crow who asked me what I was doing dreaming this dream."

Ted Kooser: "You're asking the wrong geranium."

Oprah: "Who gave you my email address?"

Jesse Ventura: "You should ask the Dalai Lama."

The Dalai Lama: "You ask funny questions."

Vachel Lindsay: "Boomlay, boomlay, boomlay, Boom."

Donald Hall: "I once put together an anthology of Midwest poetry. But no one wanted to publish it. Not even publishers in the Midwest."

Gwendolyn Brooks: "Articulated, syncopated silence."

Leon Kottke: "I never heard that played on a lead-pipe flute before."

George Kalamaras: "Wash your Ganges every day."

Laura Bush: "All poetry is American poetry."

Bucky Halker: "It sounds so much better on National steel guitar."

Mary Bradley: "I don't know anything about poetry, John. You know I like crossword puzzles."

Lorine Niedecker: "In the tiny spider dangling from the tip of this pen."

Kent Johnson: "Who can say what's poetry and what's not?"

Joan Cusack: "Who gave you my cell number?"

Billy Corgan: "Are you still trying to figure that out?"

Garrison Keillor: "There was a young poet from Winona, who was always composing a sestina, wherever he went, he added its scent, and now he delivers pizza."

Liz Phair: "You never know what you'll find in the dumpster."

Catfish Keith: "The Washed Out, Blown Away, Dried Out, What's That Smell Midwest Blues."

Maria Sabina: "Place a pinch between your cheek and gum."

John Prine: "Just cuz."

Georgia O'Keeffe: "Watch your top knot."

Ernest Hemingway: "And you yourn."

Sandra Cisneros: "The Midwest is every place. There is no such place as the Midwest."

Mavis Staple: "Honey, if I say it is, it is."

Vachel Lindsay: "Boomlay, boomlay, boomlay, Boom."

VIII

trancelumination:

to suffer from hiccups and believe it's a god or goddess fighting to be born.

Findings from the future: A Spanish scientist sleeping with a pacifier appeared to be migrating west from Canada toward Siberia. Male artists with big brains who wear sexy clothes have smaller testicles, and obese people who create a fearless mouse tend to have trouble with performing monkeys. Thought control was used to build a kilometer-high skyscraper. Bacteria love to eat noncreative people. Honda announced that prairie voles will start work this year as receptionists at an office near Tokyo. Psychologists found that anger among married guinea pigs can cause wounds to heal more slowly. The normally monogamous bones of Nicolaus Copernicus could jump the species barrier even into the next generation, and experts said the earth is unlikely to destroy violent cell phones any time soon. Venus was hard at work on a robotic snail that casts a delicate shadow on dark, promiscuous nights.

👁

One day dust shall rise and desire fall, or is it, he wondered, desire shall rise and dust fall?

👁

The world built a shed, to find shelter from the world. Then one day someone squatted in the shed and left a fetid turd.

❖

You could see he was about to go or had just returned from India. No one could tell which.

❖

We're necking in the hallway of Saint Raymond's School, leaning against the statue of the Blessed Virgin Mary, who's smashing the serpent with her bare feet. "Someone's watching us through a rifle scope. We've got to get out of here," Angelica says. Or did I say this to her? She runs down the hallway. I stand there listening to the clatter of footfall. When she gets outside, I site her in the cross hair of the rifle scope. Then I remember: Never do anything that you don't want aphorized.

❖

She told him she liked his painting: Because her cat barfed in her shoe that morning. Because she found a hair wrapped around the spout of the toothpaste tube. Because she wanted the wind to stop slamming the back door. Because the mint needed to be watered by someone missing a missing finger.

❖

A honeybee worked a hole in the sky above Globe, Arizona.

❖

My teeth hurt when crows, in *The Book of the Black Tulip*, covet my verticality.

❖

To avoid the void: carry a violin case filled with fresh dirt and open it from time to time and listen to the earth.

❖

When I told the sentence about sand trickling into our easement, it seemed strangely content. Nothing appeared more latent than the sand sleeping in the shifting firmament contained in this sentence. "You only care about the careless sand!" yelled the sentence soaked in contempt. I said I would be as content as a monument to sand if I were a sentence without intent. Oh, please don't sentence me to hearing about the motherless sand's abandonment. "In contempt of silence," said the sand, no longer confined to a sentence, no longer content with this or any other sentient arrangement. Let me leave you with this: sleep, sleek, senseless, sediment: spilling from the absolute, into and through every laden sentence.

◉

"It's a long way to Mars," she said, tracing a crease in his brow.

◉

Eroticism begins and ends with the smell of an armpit.

◉

"You're too old to be doing this shit," Grace Slick wrote me. "On the other hand," she added, "even skeletons have to have something to do."

Thirteen praises for the unpraised: 1.) The lamp in the bed has no need of shade. 2.) Pears rarely lie or tell the truth. 3.) Tripping on the reader trapped in a comma, I fell into a deep coma. 4.) As my mother would say, if you can't say something degrading, then say something nice. 5.) How was I to know my urologist would follow you into the restroom. 6.) Wind talks out of both sides of its mouth. 7.) At the poetry reading, I'm before the podium, reading from the open pizza box. There are several slices left, though I'm sure I didn't eat all the missing slices. Suddenly I realize I'm not reading a poem; I'm reading the contents of a pizza box. I freeze. Someone thirty three miles away applauds. 8.) Sand prefers to sleep with sand. 9.) Say something the trombone can't say better. 10.) "Darkness will always be larger than the United States," an aphorist in a bow tie once told me. "But not by much." 11.) I've always felt great relief when someone confuses "erratic" with "erotic." 12.) That's when I began my study of the fifty-six uses of the ketchup bottle. 13.) Warning: Reading this more than once a day may lead to sporadic truth-telling.

Only after I got off the phone with my mother did I notice the charcoal smoldering in my side.

❂

O lowly aphorism, not prose, not poem, not micro-proem. Just another belly button birthling.

❂

"But my mother said all this first," I told the audience. A small door opened in the stage floor. "Well, I never told him to say that," my mother replied, and the trapdoor closed.

❂

Leave a crumb for history's cockroach.

❂

On the last morning he lived, Mussolini took a pee.

❂

But I prefer to speak in fuscia.

❂

Dear little black ants, how is it you form these very words, and then claim you have no idea what they might say?

❂

If I sew that hole in my pocket, I'll never know what I might lose.

❂

In row after row, in identical beds with metal side bars, so the famous do not roll out of their beds as they sleep, here they are, the poets whose work I have read for years in magazines and books and anthologies. No matter their style, content, line length, side by side they lie in bed after bed, each poet sleeping in exactly the same position, right leg over left, a chorus line frozen mid-kick. I sprinkle each sleeper with a light dusting of lime, careful not to bestow upon one more than any other.

◉

This is not a dream: to find, in your friend's bathroom, a lavender bar of soap bearing your birth and death dates.

◉

Sign posted over the exit of the labyrinth: "Let us know if we can do anything to make your journey more difficult."

◉

At last, an aphorism even an aphid could love.

Not that you asked, but because you didn't ask, an author's credo: Dear Kind Reader, I can never tell who's renting out the top third of my head. At 11:11, someone will tell you it is 11:11. A toad should never be told, hot or cold, it could be towed. You know you've lost the war when one of your troops says: "We had to destroy them to make them safe." Maybe that's why on most days I believe the taxi cab driver ars poetica: "I can only know what your mouth lets me know." Lincoln licked the log so well only the log could recollect Lincoln. When I was a janitor, I smelled of disinfectant in armpit and tongue. Note the standard of perfection in the previous statement. I assure you, my faceless friend, every letter here has been borrowed from other alphabets, other writers, yet every word is certifiably my own. At 11:11, someone will say, "Now what were you saying about November 11?" Before leaving, please place your extant burden in the salt shaker. One needn't go far to know here is too near. I swear I never thought pulling on that thread dangling from your wrist would make you too disappear.

Acknowledgments

Some of the tranceluminations in this book have appeared in *American Aesthetic, Calapooya Collage, Caliban, Fault Lines, Hotel Amerika, Journal of the International Collective of Cosmic Aphorists, Kerf, Key Satch(el), Lilies and Cannonballs Review, Oval Magazine, Poetry East, Puerto del Sol, Quarter After Eight, Redactions, Sawbuck, Wolf Head Quarterly*, and the pamphlet *States of Common Rapture*, Red Pagoda Press.

With thanks to the Illuminati (those who can be named): Bonnie and Ric Amesquita, Bob and Susan Arnold, Joe and Jean Gastiger, Jay Griswold, Ray Gonzalez, Kent Johnson, George Kalamaras, Ken Letko, Becky Parfitt, Susan Porterfield, Matt Ryan, Phil Woods, and most of all, Jana.

About the Author

John Bradley was born in Brooklyn, New York, and grew up in: Munich and Nuremberg, Germany (though he claims Germanic amnesia); Framingham, Natick, and Saxonville, Massachusetts; Lincoln and Omaha, Nebraska; Massapequa and Lynbrook, New York; and Wayzata, Minnesota. For much of his childhood, his most important possession was his public library card.

His job history includes: newspaper carrier, snow shoveler, library clerk, book warehouse worker (ripping covers off returned books), dishwasher (he lasted one shift), housepainter, tea bag packer, fish habitat builder, newspaper circulation desk clerk, window washer, test monitor, bagel-sandwich-maker, copy store clerk, drawing class model, mover, bookstore clerk, poll worker, and night custodian. He regrets he was never a mail carrier.

He earned a B.A. in History and a B.A. in English from the University of Minnesota. In 1972, his draft board reluctantly granted him conscientious objector status. He received his M.A. from Colorado State University and his M.F.A. from Bowling Green State University. His book *Love-In-Idleness* (Word Works), a collection of persona poems set in Fascist Italy, won the Washington Prize. He's also authored *Terrestrial Music* (Cursbstone), *War on Words* (BlazeVOX), and *You Don't Know What You Don't Know* (CSU Poetry Center). He's edited *Atomic Ghost* (Coffee House), *Learing to Glow* (Univ. Arizona), and *Eating the Pure Light: Homage to Thomas McGrath* (Backwaters). He is the recipient of a Pushcart Prize and two NEA Fellowships in Poetry. He teaches at Northern Illinois University. He lives in DeKalb, Illinois, with his wife, Jana, a catalog librarian, and their cats, Kiki and Zuzu.

(Note: Mr. Bradley provided no endnotes or footnotes for verification of the above.)

www.ingramcontent.com/pod-product-compliance
Lightning Source LLC
LaVergne TN
LVHW011211080426
835508LV00007B/721